Forward

From Raisy Chen- BitRaise Founder

The process to achieve ICO could be demanding, many ICO's are having tough time reaching out to the right audience and ending up not reaching their financial goal. Our aim is to make ICO as comfortable as possible by helping our clients to quickly and efficiently enter the mature stage of real marketization. We achieve this through understanding the need of our clients and by establishing a reliable execution plan for them.

In the past, the only way for companies to raise funds was to issue bonds or sell their shares, the emergence of ICO gave companies a second opportunity. While IPO allows the investors to own the share and becomes a part of the company, ICO allows investors to access the services provided by the company and in return, the company can establish followers and thus free promoters and feedbacks. ICO creates a synergy between the investors and the company without the risk of interference of the management that IPO has.

However ICO has recently encountered some issues. There has been an increase incidents of ICO related frauds in the market which brought up the doubts in many investors. Majority of the ICO companies tend to be on their early round, and angel round investments are by convention, highly risky. Just like investing in angel round companies, there are several inspection methods that can be used when evaluating an ICO company, to name a few: product development, roadmap, financial model, market dynamics, and social media feedback, all these can help the investors to better evaluate an ICO company. Expert reviewed white paper as well as an well experienced operation team are also very crucial, together they can keep the plan in place and organized.

There are three types of customers we assist:

1. Enterprises with good industrial operations.

2. Large group companies whose reputation exceeds the benefits brought by ICO

3. Companies that cooperate with the government or have government licenses.

The advantage of working with these three types of customers is that raising money is not their purpose. Their main purpose of ICO is the actual application of the currency in the system. This means that these companies are seeking for assistance in risk management and consumer responsibility and that is what we are specialized in. Our purpose is to help our clients to achieve enterprise optimization, model architecture, good looping and risk management.

In conclusion, we hope to help more robust, real deal companies to become ICO and with this, we can take part to create a sound and healthy block chain ecosystem that would lead to common prosperity.

Table of Contents

1 How to invest ICO?
- 1.1 What is an ICO?
- 1.2 Antiquity of ICOs
- 1.3 Legal Status of ICOs
- 1.4 Benefits of ICO
  - 1.4.1 Democratization
  - 1.4.2 Immense Potential of Profit
- 1.5 Main Issues with ICO
  - 1.5.1 Lack of Supervisory Oversight
  - 1.5.2 Lack of Track Record

2 **A Guide for ICO Investment: Learn how to contribute to ICOs?**
- 2.1 Research on Future ICOs
- 2.2 Due Diligence
- 2.3 Participation Procedure for ICO
  - 2.3.1 Open one Exchange Account
  - 2.3.2 Open Wallets to Partake in ICOs
  - 2.3.3 Follow the Instructions of ICO
  - 2.3.4 Exchanges to Successfully Trade ICO Coins
- 2.4 What is the difference between wallets and Exchanges and why you can't invest ICO through Exchanges?
- 2.5 Start With A Coinbase
- 2.6 Set up MyEtherWallet
- 2.7 Ideas to Secure Your Private Key
- 2.8 Researching and Finding ICOs
  - 2.8.1 LEAST
- 2.9 Which Exchange will it launch? When?

- 2.10 Understand Funding Types
  - 2.10.1 Open-end Mutual Fund:
  - 2.10.2 ETF (Exchange-traded Fund)
  - 2.10.3 CEFs (Closed-end Fund)
- 2.11 Foundation behind a Crypto Index Tactic

3 Background
- 3.1 What is Cryptocurrency?
- 3.2 What is blockchain?
- 3.3 What is Ethereum?
- 3.4 What are smart contracts?

4 What is ERC-20?
- 4.1 What is an ERC-20 compliant token?
- 4.2 Benefits
- 4.3 How to create ERC-20 Token?
  - 4.3.1 Decide Your Tokens
  - 4.3.2 Contract Code
  - 4.3.3 Use TestNet to Test Tokens
  - 4.3.4 Custom Token
  - 4.3.5 Verify a Source Code
  - 4.3.6 On Main Net

Conclusion

Acknowledge

1 How to invest ICO?

1.1 What is an ICO?

ICO means initial coin offerings is a great fundraising mechanism in which companies sell their crypto tokens in interchange for ether and bitcoin. It is similar to IPO (initial public offering) that requires investors to buy shares of an organization.

The new phenomenon of ICOs is quickly becoming famous within the community of blockchain. Several people consider that ICO projects are unregulated securities that enable funds to increase unjustified capital. For other people, it is an innovation in the venture-funding traditional model. The SEC (securities and exchange commission) of the United States has concluded the status of issued token in notorious ICO DAO. It has forced several investors and projects to reexamine the models of funding of several ICOs.

The Howey test is an essential criterion to consider trustable token. It should be treated security and subject to particular restrictions imposed by SEC. It is easy to structure ICOs because of ERC-20 token standards. These tokens abstract several development processes essential to create one new cryptographic asset. Some ICOs work by letting investors send funds to smart contracts those funds, stores and distributes an equivalent worth in new tokens at a future point.

There are some restrictions on participants for their contribution in the ICOs, assuming that the token is not a security. You are taking money from a worldwide pool of investors, and the amounts increased in ICOs may be astronomical. The ICOs have fundamental issues, and most of them increase pre-product money. It can make the investment risky and extremely speculative. There is an argument about the fundraising style, and it is useful to incentivize the development of the protocol.

1.2 Antiquity of ICOs

Different projects used crowdsale prototypes to get funds for their development in 2013. Ripple pre-mind one billion tokens of XRP and sold them to interested investors for bitcoin and fiat currencies. Ethereum increases a little over dollar 18 million in 2014.

The first attempt was DAO at fundraising for new tokens on Ethereum. Actually, it promised the creation of a decentralized organization that would provide funds to blockchain projects. Different token holders made this unique governance decision. The DAO successfully raised money over dollar 150 million. Unknown attackers drained millions because of technical vulnerabilities. To avoid these vulnerabilities, the foundation of Ethereum used the best action to move forward with one hard fork. It allows them to claw their stolen funds back.

The initial attempt for the safety of tokens on an Ethereum platform was unsuccessful. Developers of blockchain realized that the use of Ethereum to launch one token was easy than pursuing seed rounds via the typical endeavor capital model. The standard ERC-20 increases the convenience of developers to create their cryptographic tokens on blockchain Ethereum.

Some people argue that crowdfunding projects can be a killer application for Ethereum and give frequency and sheer size of ICOs. Aragon raised almost $25 million in 15 minutes. Token of essential attention raised nearly $35 million in 30 seconds and Status.im raised nearly $270 million in some hours. With the convenience of use and some regulations, the ICO climates have under scrutiny from several in the community and regulatory bodies in the world.

1.3 Legal Status of ICOs

ICOs legally exist in gray areas because arguments may be made for the unfettered financial assets. The recent decision of SEC has managed to clear up some gray area. In several cases, the token is only a utility token and it allows owners to get access to a particular network or protocol. It may not classify as financial securities. If a token is one equity token, the only purpose is to escalate in value and looks like securities.

Several individuals buy tokens to get access to the fundamental platform at a point in the future. It can be difficult to disprove an idea that several token purchases are related to a speculative investment purpose. It is easy to ascertain specified the estimation figures for several projects that have released one commercial product.

The decision of SEC may provide some lucidity to the utility status and security tokens. There is sufficient room to test the limitations of legalities. For the current time, and until additional regulatory restrictions are imposed, entrepreneurs may continue to get the advantage of the new phenomenon.

1.4 Benefits of ICO

1.4.1 Democratization

ICOs allow projects to evade the customary technique of asking venture and banks capitalists that can take lots of resources and time. Anyone may invest and earn the huge returns like how big lads are familiarized to. Investing money in ICOs can be a risky venture.

1.4.2 Immense Potential of Profit

Several in this space need to invest in the Bitcoin and potentially riding the wave of purchasing coins at pennies on dollars and selling them at an astral valuation. Several ICOs have a theoretical white paper with some or no proof of concept. Validating the potential of high payoff because of the extreme risk taken by investors.

1.5 Main Issues with ICO

1.5.1 Lack of Supervisory Oversight

Supervisory are suitable in the protection of investors and people. The market of ICO is unfettered and may attract bad performers that are scammers, manipulative and fraudulent. Through ICO, you can easily raise money. You have to write one white paper and ready to go. It is important to be careful and have due assiduousness before investment.

1.5.2 Lack of Track Record

Several ICOs may not have working products and a conceptual white paper outlines the working method of coin. ICOs are asking for large funding amount. For example, the biggest ICOs was current Tezos crowdsale that netted a $232 million shopping. Valuation doesn't exist in a customary setting.

2 A Guide for ICO Investment: Learn how to contribute to ICOs?

2.1 Research on Future ICOs

Pay attention on the outlets or resources that features the advanced ICOs. Knowing the current ICOs for advance planning, especially for ICOs that has one whitelist. The whitelist ICO requires advance registration to participate in ICOs that are hallmarks of famous ICOs with limited coins.

2.2 Due Diligence

It is important to perform your research to ascertain that the ICO has good reputation. Several main factors should be considered for effective assessment of ICO. You have to look at analysis and reviews done by other people to authenticate the prospective of ICO. The good review resources of ICO include:

Reddit: Particular channels feature reviews of ICO done by different community members like ethtrader, icocrypto, cryptocurrency.

Crush Crypto: It is a website dedicated to evaluate ICOs through thorough fundamental analysis

2.3 Participation Procedure for ICO

If you want to participate in the procedure for ICO, you have to follow these procedures:

2.3.1 Open one Exchange Account

If you are confident to perform your research and interested to proceed with participating in the initial public offerings, you have to open one fiat-accepting exchange cryptocurrency account to convert a national fiat currency in famous BTC (cryptocurrency of Bitcoin) or ETH (Ether).

2.3.2 Open Wallets to Partake in ICOs

It is important to have your wallets. An exchange account like Kraken, Bittrex and Poloniex doesn't count as your personal wallet because you can't get control to their personal keys. Participant in the ICO needs you to send ETH or BTC from private and personal wallets. If you can send it from exchange, you may not get tokens of ICO because the transfer originates from an exchange wallet and theoretically you don't own wallets in exchange.

You can use Ether as your base cryptocurrency because several coins of ICO are acquiescent with ERC-20 Ethereum standard and several convenient MyEtherWallet (MEW).

2.3.3 Follow the Instructions of ICO

ICOs will come with a systematic guide for participation in the ICOs. You must join a channel of official communication like Telegram or Slack to receive direct updates and ask direct questions of developing team.

2.3.4 Exchanges to Successfully Trade ICO Coins

If you trust in tech and hold the coins for medium – long-term or until you hit a price target (e.g., 2x, 3x, and 10x of capital). In case, you want to flip these coins, wait until you reaches the exchange that typically lists on ICO. Otherwise, if you have missed an ICO, you may purchase it at exchanges. See the list of common exchanges with a tendency of ICO coins list:

Ether Delta: It is a decentralized exchange. It is the first exchange to list freshly issued coins of ICO. Trade on this platform may be complex for beginners. It is not recommended for beginners.

Liqui.io: This exchange often lists latest ICO coins. It has almost 200 listed coins.

Bittrex: It is the biggest exchange of cryptocurrency by volume that accepts deposits of coin. It is the big league that each ICO has to be listed on this platform.

Poloniex: It is the second biggest exchange of cryptocurrency by volume that only needs coin deposits. This exchange has great demand among ICOs, but the criteria to become a part of Poloniex listing is extremely difficult and it has only a few coins.

Binance: This is a chain-based ICO exchange that gained great traction. It becomes the 10th largest ICO exchange by volume in just four months. It contains new consumer demands for coins.

2.4 What is the difference between wallets and Exchanges and why you can't invest ICO through Exchanges?

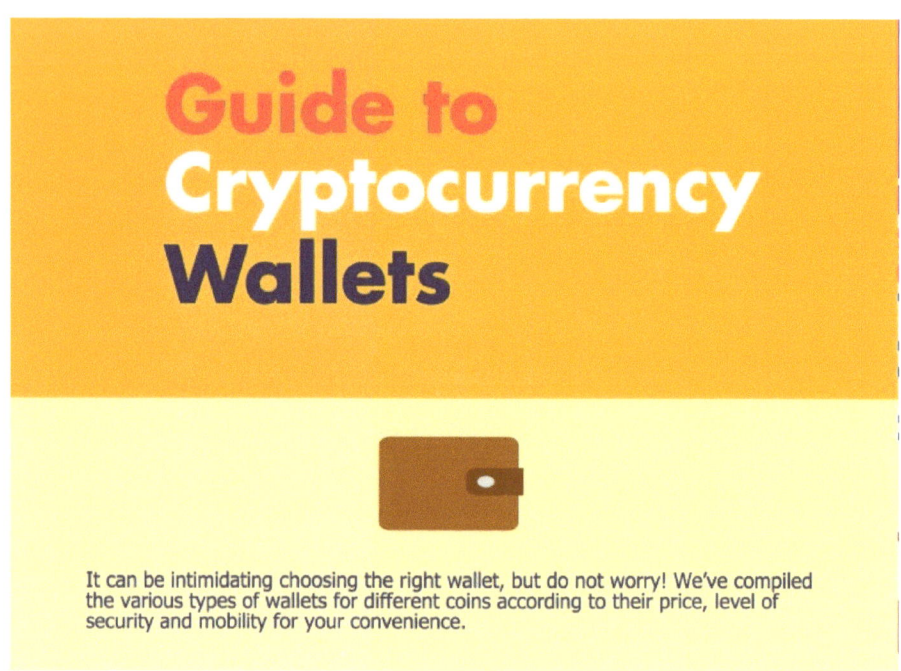

You may consider exchanges to invest, but you must avoid it. Although, will automatically get a wallet as you open one exchange account or a wallet hosted by exchange. You will not have control of public and private keys. Having the control of keys means getting full control of coins. Exchanges may work like banks and it is a 3rd party service provider to keep your coins safe.

Exchanges can be shut-down or hacked, result in the loss of your coins. The exchanges have lack of controlling framework on cryptocurrencies. Your wallet offers you the maximum control.

Moreover, participation in ICOs need you to have private wallets from which you can invest. You can't invest in an ICO through an exchange account.

You may find it intimidating to choose the right wallet, but there is no need to worry. Wallets are available for different coins as per their mobility, security level and price. Here is a list of wallets for your guidance:

Bitcoin Wallets

Wallet-type	Wallet Services	Pricing	Security	Mobility
Exchange-hosted	Accepts Fiat Deposits (USD): Coinbase/Gemini/ Kraken/GDAX/Bitstamp /Cex.io/ Only Accepts Coin Deposits: Poloniex/Bittrex/ Bitfinex/Liqui	Free	Different exchanges have different layers of security. Only Coinbase has 100% insurance.	Web-based
Online	Blockchain.info	Free	Very secure. Uses multiple security layers on the server side.	Web-based
Paper Wallet	Bitcoinpaperwallet.com bitaddress.org	Free	Safe from online hackers. Level of security depends on how and where the paper is stored.	Traditional cold storage

Ethereum Wallets

Wallet-type	Wallet Services	Pricing	Security	Mobility
Exchange-hosted	Accepts Fiat Deposits (USD): Coinbase/Gemini/ Kraken/GDAX/Cex.io Only Accepts Coin Deposits: Poloniex/Bittrex/ Bitfinex/Liqui	Free	Different exchanges have different layers of security. Only Coinbase has 100% insurance.	Web-based
Online	MyEtherWallet.com	Free	Very secure. The wallet creation process occurs on your computer; MEW doesn't have servers to store your information. You have to personally back up all the wallet information to secure it	Web-based
Paper Wallet	EthAddress (https://ryepdx.github.io/ethaddress.org/#/)	Free	All data saved on piece of paper. Totally safe from online hackers. Level of offline security depends on how and where the paper is stored.	Traditional cold storage

Bitcoin & Ethereum Hardware Wallets

	Pricing	Security	Mobility
Ledger Nano S	USD 60	Highest Security. Uses two secure elements/chips.	Portable, thumbdrive-like
	USD 99	Highest Security. Leverages on Trezor's code and software.	Portable, thumbdrive-like
	USD 99	Highest Security. Touted as the gold standard for hardware wallets.	Portable, thumbdrive-like

ERC-20 refers to the standard protocol within the Ethereum blockchain, listing down a common set of rules for tokens to follow. This ensures the interoperability between the different type of tokens within the Ethereum blockchain, enabling seamless interaction with smart contracts and decentralized applications on the network.

Examples of ERC-20 Coins

1) Golem - A decentralised global market for computing power

2) Basic Attention Token (BAT) - A new token for the digital advertising industry

3) Aragon - Aragon lets you manage entire organizations using the blockchain. This makes Aragon organizations more efficient than their traditional counterparties.

Wallets For ERC-20 Coins

Wallet-type	Wallet Services	Pricing	Security	Mobility
Exchange-hosted	Only Accepts Coin Deposits: Poloniex/Bittrex/Liqui	Free	Different exchanges have different layers of security. Only Coinbase has 100% insurance.	Web-based
Online	MyEtherWallet.com	Free	Very secure. The wallet creation process occurs on your computer; MEW doesn't have servers to store your information. You have to personally back up all the wallet information to secure it.	Web-based

Wallet for other alternative Coins

Wallet-type	Wallet Services	Pricing	Security	Mobility
Exchange-hosted	Only Accepts Coin Deposits: Poloniex/Bittrex/Liqui	Free	Different exchanges have different layers of security. Only Coinbase has 100% insurance.	Web-based

2.5 Start With A Coinbase

Before investing in the ICOs, you should purchase Ethereum. The places to buy Ethereum (ETH) with dollars are limited. The easy and default route is the use of coinbase. The company get the advantage of its position as early entrants. The hype of Bitcoin is skyrocketed and Coinbase gained disproportional reward by becoming an early player.

You can get the advantage of other options like Gemini, owned by twin brothers from Facebook saga. While fee of Gemini is lower and it may take some days to complete the purchasing of a coin, that is an eternity in crypto market. The price changes may take some minutes.

Coinbase is not good in terms of the speed of transaction. Sometimes, the delays may be because of slow networks that confirms the transaction. It is because of maintenance on the side of Coinbase. Fears are growing in a community that Coinbase use for manipulation of prices because they have a large share of market among different companies. These companies bridge dollars to cryptocurrency.

Here are some options to purchase Ethereum or Bitcoin with dollars:

- **Coinbase:** Convenient to use, market leader and has a mobile app
- **Gemini:** It is an ideal option, but with some limitations

2.6 Set up MyEtherWallet

The ICOs are based on smart contracts Ethereum and your wallet must support receiving of tokens. During ICO, you may send Ethereum to a company issuing one new token and receiving the token amount based on the announced rate of exchange.

For instance, the exchange rate of the company is ETH = 1,000 X coins. The market of ICO is similar to the wild west and there is no set of policies and rules. Companies often issues the limits of ICO for people to purchase the coins.

It seems strange to set up MyEtherWallet for the first time because you will not get a username. You will create one passport and download a Keystone file, often mentioned as one private key. MyEtherWallet produces one public address for your private key and wallet. It will become an easy way to access the wallet. The public address is unidentified, but each person in a network may see it. In simple words, each person may see transactions that happen in a wallet but no one recognizes that it is yours.

For instance, Bob wishes to send Ethereum (money) to Jimmy. First, the Jimmy has to know the account number of bank (wallet or public address). Account number of Jimmy is 1325. Bon sends 1 Ethereum ($1) to the account of John. Every person in the network may see that an account number 1325 has received 1 Ethereum ($1). Now jimmy will need his private key to access this wallet, bank account to send or withdraw Ethereum. If Jimmy loses a private key, he can't access his wallet (bank account) and money will be gone forever.

For this reason, it is essential to secure a private key. Unlike the login of your bank account that you may reset by showing your personal identity or with identification issued by state, a compromised or lost keys are important for everyone.

2.7 Ideas to Secure Your Private Key

Here are some methods to secure a private key, such as hardware wallet. One hardware wallet will be an encrypted device to store private keys for your personal coins. You may store encrypted key on your flash drive and manage it in your secure box at your bank as backup. It is possible to use encryption software, such as a password to store a private key. If you are regularly trading, you have to frequently access your key; hence, encryption software can be a safe choice.

2.8 Researching and Finding ICOs

It may be difficult to find out an ICO. You can find the best option y analyzing a white paper that is available with ICO. For your convenience, here is a unique ICO LEAST:

2.8.1 LEAST
L: Logical

A white paper is a powerful tool because it contains educative content. This document determines the technology of the blockchain project. The file contains a comprehensive description of the structure architecture and interactions with the users and current market data, requirements to issue and use tokens, and growth anticipations. Moreover, it offers a list of team members, advisors and investors of the project. Our job is to confirm if the contents of the whitepaper is logical or not.

Sometime the early items would even come into the market and claim their white paper to be announced. Without a white paper, it could be difficult for the team of a project to perform a successful procedure of ICO. People who are interested in investing in the project will lack proper information about the technology and business experience of team members.

E: Essential

A token is a particular amount of digital resources that you can control and reassign control of tokens to someone. In some projects, customized tokens are essential because these projects are handled for funding with a token, such as Ethereum or Bitcoin. These kinds of projects need their tokens for the separate offering.

As people invest in ICO projects, they are supporting the particular projects and anticipate that the value of a project will increase with time. Hence, these projects give an appropriate return on investment. If a project obtains funding via Bitcoin or Ethereum, the ROI (return on investment) would be linked to the performance of cryptocurrencies and project will not get funds.

A: Alliance

A token is a new term for a privately issued currency. Usually, sovereign administrations issue currency and adjust its governance and conditions; in spirit directing how an economy works with cash as the exchange average for value. In the presence of the blockchain, you have new organizations who are issuing their digital money as a cryptocurrency. This digital money has an alliance with their own rules and terms around its operations. Mini self-sustainable economies create it.

S: Structure

Several factors affect the failure and success of ICOs, and the composition of a team is one of these factors. The structure of the team plays a vital role in the entire operation. Founder or CEO is the main inspirational source. The CEO is responsible for describing his vision for starting an ICO project. After CEO, chief operating officer and chief technology officer play essential roles. They must have excellent managerial skills and experience to take the responsibilities of technical teams.

Moreover, the CFO (chief financial officer) is responsible for managing the finances of the company. Developers are the core of a prosperous ICO team. These people work on whole technology to make your digital currency live.

T: Trade

The primary purpose of coins or tokens is to endorse diversification of volatile cryptocurrency market. It allows investors to invest in the whole space of cryptocurrency without any trouble of investing in numerous exchanges or wallets. The high volume of coins in the cryptocurrency market may decrease the value of some coins over others. You must have advisers and marketing personnel in your team to make your ICOs trade successful.

2.9 Which Exchange will it launch? When?

The main goal of coin is to manage index funding of the particular coins that have an average weight of the top 30 coins available in this market. The value of top performing coins may be subjective, but the ICOs only wants to decrease the investment risk while increasing the return of investors. This will increase the interest of people in the investment.

In this situation, the creation of un-correlated or negatively collected coins with highest possible return and chances of substituting coins with the 30 top indexes is essential. Some highly unpredictable coins and highly correlated can't be ignored with the non-zero likelihood of spontaneous failure. Investors can get the advantage of competing matrices to optimize their portfolio to earn expected a return and decrease unpredictability at the same time. Hence, coins want to maximize the Sharpe ratio that is described as a ration of the expected return of a portfolio over the portfolios with typical deviation rate.

An imitation of millions of probable single market costs is conducted for the selection procedure. This procedure is centered on the prominent historic correlation and unpredictability of returns. The figures from the data of past 12 months were correlated. Moreover, a forfeit is utilized on new coins with minimum previous data and maximum chances of impetuous failure with a patented scoring function that is centered on the lindy effect. This effect states that the chances of failure or expectation of future life is relative to endure while trends tend to fade quickly.

Subsequently, coins that have a longer historical data have good chances of getting almost zero impulsive failure, although the new coins available in the market have low volume and high probability of impulsively becoming worthless. The chances that a coin may fail in only one day is defined by the circulation proportion of coins, sentiment, longevity and market cap.

A report is produced during imitation procedure that contains possible Sharpe ratio, maximum draw-dawn, possible return, expected return or loss 95th percentile and maximum days of return. The optimization procedure proves helpful in the development of optimal portfolio with the use of a generic algorithm. This portfolio is substituted after every simulation via the procedure of up-weighting high performing assets and down-weighting assets that have poor performance until the production of a portfolio with optimum assets via future settings to increase the returns and decrease impulsiveness. This portfolio is reweighted repeatedly to find the new high performer in the current market and remove all the lower performers from this list.

Assets that were expected to fail because of hacking or frauds are also expelled from this list to offer maximum opportunities to top performing coins. Rebalancing of numbers on this list is triggered by information and schedule. When information is there for the failure of a particular coin, there must be a rebalancing of stable assets. The rebalancing of portfolios is occurred after seven days as per a schedule. Although, adjustment of overall balance of index and full scope audit is scheduled to do annually.

Without any doubt, the coins have numerous benefits, such as convenience, zero exit fee, zero broker fees, full control, low price bound and maximum transparency. Instead of keeping your token to a centralized platform, you can sell them or even exchange them without any restriction. Automation allows the exchange to operate with 0.5% P/A fee as compared to average 3% P/A fees of the market. No one will doubt the capability of human traders and administrators. Fortunately, an index fund approach is free from any judgment or discretion, just observance of a particular method is determined by data science. The total quantity of tokens, asset weighting, and rebalancing frequency was determined and this approach is detailed in our White Paper.

The ICO funds are used to purchase the fundamental assets. Tokens may be liquidated via C20 smart contract for their particular share in the NAV (net asset value) of the portfolio. This is essential for the protection of the cost of token because it may not be sensible to trade at the lowest possible value of exchange when these tokens may be directly settled for their higher value.

Funds with astral presentation appeal substantial amounts of money. A manager may use this new money to pursue some coins. The buying pressure may increase the prices and force the managers to pay maximum prices than the usual. It may affect all token holders by decrease the future gains of the funds. This may become the motivation for issuing no tokens post-ICO and immediately create the value of contributors.

Coin can be beneficial for the whole community because the liquidity and transparency of market will increase with trading activity. It will increase understanding, funding, and support to the trading activity. Traditional investors with uncertainty about investment in a single system or technology may have support option of emerging cryptocurrencies market via a reliable channel.

2.10 Understand Funding Types

2.10.1 Open-end Mutual Fund:
This fund issues unlimited investment share in bonds or stocks. Investment increase opportunities of shares where selling share may take them away from circulation. Shares are traded on demand at their total value that is based on the value of underlying securities of the fund. It is calculated after finishing a trading day. After redeeming a large volume of shares, the funds may sell some investments to make payment to investors. Fund administration is necessary to bring shares.

2.10.2 ETF (Exchange-traded Fund)
These funds are similar to open-end mutual funds, but these are traded as a common stock. One can't purchase them directly from fund administration. These are traded at a discount or premium to NAV, but this is short-lived because of arbitrage by institutional investors.

2.10.3 CEFs (Closed-end Fund)
These funds are seeded once-off through an IPO and later on traded on an exchange. Further shares are not issued and the closed-end funds have no influence on fundamental assets.

The structure of token is correspondent to a hybrid type, such as CHF that is a closed-end fund to trade with a particular index strategy whereas all closed-end traditional funds are actively accomplished.

Post-ICO investors may be able to buy tokens on the exchange. No other tokens can be directly sold. Selling and purchasing tokens on exchanges may not affect the fundamental CHFs and NAV. They can be traded at an exceptional based on the force of the market.

The liquidation options prove helpful to create a price floor in smart contracts and efficiently ensure that the tokens can't be traded at any discount.

2.11 Foundation behind a Crypto Index Tactic

Index investment shows outstanding growth among investors since the initial index fund was introduced in 1976. This was a successful form of low-cost investment that allows outperformance of index funds to a number of active manager across asset styles and market.

Investment horizon of more than 10 years proves that the 80% management of the large-cap funds failed to overtake their particular benchmark index. The chances of picking a persuasive fund manager are low as the studies show the virtually random comparison of future performance and past performance.

With an index fund, investors can trail the index and the basic trends behind the assortment of assets without relying on any particular trend or asset. Active trading is missing apart from rebalancing all assets at the intervals of fixed time. This proves helpful for the funds to constantly track the performance of mean market even after seeing the fall out of original assets.

The tokenized portfolio of token may be the 1st of its type and it is purchased with crypto and holds cryptocurrencies. It is good to bring old-economy money and stability in an ecosystem that can boost liquid and offer a consistent instrument for all those people who considered it was risky to invest in one technology.

It is assumed that a person can't attribute the shortage of cryptocurrency acceptance through retail investors seeking for the allocation of high-risk funds in the portfolio to the exertion of buying cryptocurrencies. The payment methods, exchange services and methods to buy cryptocurrencies is exponentially increasing. In numerous cases, it is less burdensome and easy to buy bitcoin as compared to investment in the USD denominated common funds.

The writers believe that the deficiency of investment can be because of the fact that no products were available and communicate efficiently in non-technical plain language and discernable to the sector. Unacceptable risks and high risks are different in the thoughts of numerous investors. Tokens aims to take the risk to a new level for the allocation to the portfolio of a trade investor.

3 Background

3.1 What is Cryptocurrency?

A cryptocurrency is a digital asset envisioned to be utilized as an exchange medium in a similar way like conventional currencies are. They are considered as assets by investors who are expecting to increase the value of cryptocurrency over time. Cryptocurrencies are contingent upon the cryptography utilized within the blockchain; the method in which the cryptography is utilized beside particular other protocols confirms that these particular assets have features desirable in the digital currency (immutability, transferability, and security).

3.2 What is blockchain?

A blockchain is an incessantly growing list of records known as blocks that are secured and linked using cryptography. Every block consists of a cryptographic hash that links it to the previous block, transaction data and timestamp. The blockchain is designed in a way to make a modification of data impossible. In this distributed and open ledger, transaction is recorded efficiently between two parties in a permanent and verifiable manner.

3.3 What is Ethereum?

In terms of its functionality and capabilities, it is the most advanced form of blockchain launched in 2015. It expedites the functioning of decentralized applications. A direct link of cryptocurrency to the Ethereum is called Ether. It is known as the life-blood of Blockchain and required for numerous transactions in the network.

3.4 What are smart contracts?

These are programs run completely on the blockchain Ethereum. This network is accessible to anyone having a computer. Anyone is allowed to deploy and write code to smart contracts and once this program runs on the blockchain, it will simultaneously run on thousands of computer in the world. The capabilities and properties of each program are unambiguous earlier by the person who coded it. These contracts can implement any kind of program. These are used to keep track and issue your own cryptocurrencies, such as Ethereum Token. This is an important part of this great ecosystem. For instance, banking services, operating betting, escrow services, etc.

4 What is ERC-20?

The coin will be depended on the blockchain Ethereum platform. These coins may have the similar level of security and technology advancement just like Ethereum or Bitcoin. Basically, ERC-20 is Ethereum token standard used for the smart contracts of Ethereum. ERC20 defines a list of common rules that are important to implement on an Ethereum token. It gives an ability to developers to program the function of new tokens within Ethereum ecosystem. The protocol of token is famous for crowdfunding companies through ICO (Initial Coin Offering).

4.1 What is an ERC-20 compliant token?

ERC means Ethereum Request for Comments and it is an authorized protocol to propose improvements to an Ethereum network 20. ERC20 defines some rules that should be followed for the acceptance of a token known as an ERC20 token. Basically, 20 is the ID number on Ethereum network. All tokens follow standard rules and these rules must be followed by tokens for the interactions with each other on the network. These tokens are assets of blockchain with some value that you can send and receive like Ethereum, Litecoin, and Bitcoin.

4.2 Benefits

ICOs offer numerous benefits, such as no fees of a broker, convenience, zero exit fee, full control, lower price and full transparency. Instead of bounding your tokens on a central platform, you can easily exchange or sell your tokens without any limitation. Automation enables token provider to operate with 0.5% p/a fees as compared to 3% p/a of the market rate.

There is no need to worry about the ability of human fund traders/administrators. The index fund stratagem is free from judgment or discretion, just stick to a particular method through data science. The asset weightings, rebalancing frequency, and token numbers were cautiously determined and we have a detailed approach in our white paper.

The ICO funds are good to purchase underlying assets. Tokens may be liquidated via C20 smart contract for their particular share of NAV (net asset value) of the portfolio. It is important for the protection of token price because it is not good to sell at the limited price on the exchange when tokens may be directly liquidated for a greater value.

The stellar performance of funds can attract a considerable amount of money. A manager will like to use the new money to "chase" a small cluster of coins. Buying pressure on coins can drive their prices up and force the fund administrator to pay higher costs. This situation can affect all token holders by decreasing the future gains of the fund. This will become motivation for issuing no tokens post-ICO.

The actual market cap of the S&P 500 (30th June 2017) was 21.83 trillion USD and the whole combined market cap of cryptocurrency is a fraction, such as 0.7%. The S&P 500 is a tiny part of the global investment market. These have particular potential to familiarize retail investors in the crypto market.

Crypto exposure returns with a limited risk broad profile and offers a persuasive case to fiat and crypto investors. The value proposition of token (diversification of each token) will be promoted through investor and marketing outreach. These tokens can be purchased post-ICO on exchange from the participants of ICO and highlight the real demand for decreased risk investments of crypto whilst instantaneously creating value for contributors.

These tokens are beneficial for the community in terms of liquidity and market transparency and results of trading activity can increase these benefits. We offer fresh funding, understanding, and support to the community. Traditional investors with some uncertainties about investment in a single system or technology will have support options in the emerging market of cryptocurrency.

Investors have seen exponential growth in index investment after the launch of 1st index mutual funds in 1976. It is a successful type of investment with low-cost for the outperformance of index funds across asset styles and market.

Investment horizon of more than 10-year demonstrates that 80% of the large-cap fund administrators failed to overtake their particular benchmark index. The chances of choosing a winning manager are really low. As per some studies, the future performance is random as compared to past performance.

Index funds prove good for investors to track an index, a fundamental trend after the assortment of assets without being contingent on a specific one. High-volume traders can exploit pricing for the impairment of the public by starting sell-offs that cataract and result in flash smashes so that people can buy the tokens at cheap rates. The liquidation opportunities offer a protection for floor price to ensure that the cost should not drop below the value of underlying assets as a result of market manipulation. There is no guarantee about prices because these may freely increase because the hypothetical value is generated by heavy demand for a cheap price, automated portfolio of cryptocurrency and diversification.

Dynamically allocated a small percentage of digital assets may held via smart contracts in ether to simplify liquidation option. This percentage can be controlled as usage demands. The majority of cryptocurrency assets may be available in different cold loading wallets.

At the time of withdrawal, the ICO tokens can be transferred back to managers. These are resold in exchange at present NAV for each token or market rate that is higher. The primary assets may be rebought with the help of liquidation options that may be due to market rate floor.

4.3 How to create ERC-20 Token?

Programming with Ethereum can be a really challenging. It is new to with overflow responses and documentation. You can create your Ethereum token in one hour so you can utilize it for your projects. Here are instructions to create ERC-20 token. The creation procedure is free from fancy rules.

4.3.1 Decide Your Tokens

If you want to create your ERC-20 tokens, you must have the following:

Name of token

Symbol of token

Decimal places of token

Total tokens (number) in circulation

For the private coins, you may choose:

Name: Private Coins

Symbol: ???

Total Tokens in Circulation: 100,0000

Decimal Places: 0

Decimal places is for tricky things. Several tokens have 18 or more decimal places, it means that you have almost .000000000000000001 tokens.

When you create token, you have to be careful about decimal places and how these decimals fit in the larger image of a project.

For this example, we will keep everything simple and need people to have one token or not. There is nothing between so we choose 0. You may choose 1 if you need people to have half of a token or 18 for standard.

4.3.2 Contract Code

You can copy and paste this contract to create ERC-20 token. The Source code is "TokenFactory"

pragma solidity ^0.4.4;

contract Token {

```
/// @return total amount of tokens
function totalSupply() constant returns (uint256 supply) {}


/// @param _owner The address from which the balance will be retrieved
/// @return The balance
function balanceOf(address _owner) constant returns (uint256 balance) {}


/// @notice send `_value` token to `_to` from `msg.sender`
/// @param _to The address of the recipient
/// @param _value The amount of token to be transferred
/// @return Whether the transfer was successful or not
function transfer(address _to, uint256 _value) returns (bool success) {}


/// @notice send `_value` token to `_to` from `_from` on the condition it is approved by `_from`
/// @param _from The address of the sender
/// @param _to The address of the recipient
/// @param _value The amount of token to be transferred
```

/// @return Whether the transfer was successful or not

function transferFrom(address _from, address _to, uint256 _value) returns (bool success) {}

/// @notice `msg.sender` approves `_addr` to spend `_value` tokens

/// @param _spender The address of the account able to transfer the tokens

/// @param _value The amount of wei to be approved for transfer

/// @return Whether the approval was successful or not

function approve(address _spender, uint256 _value) returns (bool success) {}

/// @param _owner The address of the account owning tokens

/// @param _spender The address of the account able to transfer the tokens

/// @return Amount of remaining tokens allowed to spent

function allowance(address _owner, address _spender) constant returns (uint256 remaining) {}

event Transfer(address indexed _from, address indexed _to, uint256 _value);

event Approval(address indexed _owner, address indexed _spender, uint256 _value);

}

contract StandardToken is Token {

function transfer(address _to, uint256 _value) returns (bool success) {

//Default assumes totalSupply can't be over max (2^256 - 1).

//If your token leaves out totalSupply and can issue more tokens as time goes on, you need to check if it doesn't wrap.

//Replace the if with this one instead.

//if (balances[msg.sender] >= _value && balances[_to] + _value > balances[_to]) {

if (balances[msg.sender] >= _value && _value > 0) {

```
            balances[msg.sender] -= _value;
            balances[_to] += _value;
            Transfer(msg.sender, _to, _value);
            return true;
        } else { return false; }
    }

    function transferFrom(address _from, address _to, uint256 _value) returns (bool success) {
        //same as above. Replace this line with the following if you want to protect against wrapping uints.
        //if (balances[_from] >= _value && allowed[_from][msg.sender] >= _value && balances[_to] + _value > balances[_to]) {
        if (balances[_from] >= _value && allowed[_from][msg.sender] >= _value && _value > 0) {
            balances[_to] += _value;
            balances[_from] -= _value;
            allowed[_from][msg.sender] -= _value;
            Transfer(_from, _to, _value);
            return true;
        } else { return false; }
    }

    function balanceOf(address _owner) constant returns (uint256 balance) {
        return balances[_owner];
    }

    function approve(address _spender, uint256 _value) returns (bool success) {
        allowed[msg.sender][_spender] = _value;
        Approval(msg.sender, _spender, _value);
        return true;
```

```solidity
    }

    function allowance(address _owner, address _spender) constant returns (uint256 remaining) {
        return allowed[_owner][_spender];
    }

    mapping (address => uint256) balances;
    mapping (address => mapping (address => uint256)) allowed;
    uint256 public totalSupply;
}


//name this contract whatever you'd like
contract ERC20Token is StandardToken {

    function () {
        //if ether is sent to this address, send it back.
        throw;
    }

    /* Public variables of the token */

    /*
    NOTE:
    These are optional variable vanities. There is no need to include them.
        They allow you to customize the contract of token and in zero way influences the main functionality.
        Some interfaces/wallets may not bother to look at these details.
    */
```

```
    string public name;                    //fancy name: eg Simon Bucks
    uint8 public decimals;                 //How many decimals to show. ie. There could
1000 base units with 3 decimals. Meaning 0.980 SBX = 980 base units. It's like comparing 1 wei
to 1 ether.
    string public symbol;                  //An identifier: eg SBX
    string public version = 'H1.0';        //human 0.1 standard. Just an arbitrary versioning
scheme.


//
// modify these values for your own token
//
//you should ensure that name of this function should match the name of contract. For instance, if
the token is known as TutorialToken, you should mention //name of contract above as "Tutorial
Token" instead of an ERC-20 token.
    function ERC20Token(
        ) {
        balances[msg.sender] = NUMBER_OF_TOKENS_HERE;                    // Give
the creator all initial tokens (100000 for example)
        totalSupply = NUMBER_OF_TOKENS_HERE;                             //
Update total supply (100000 for example)
        name = "NAME OF YOUR TOKEN HERE";
// Set the name for display purposes
        decimals = 0;                                // Amount of decimals for display
purposes
        symbol = "SYM";                              // Set the symbol for display
purposes
    }


    /* Approves and finally calls the receiving contract */
    function approveAndCall(address _spender, uint256 _value, bytes _extraData) returns (bool
success) {
        allowed[msg.sender][_spender] = _value;
        Approval(msg.sender, _spender, _value);
```

//call the receiveApproval function on the contract you want to be notified. This crafts the function signature manually so one doesn't have to include a contract in here just for this.

//receiveApproval(address _from, uint256 _value, address _tokenContract, bytes _extraData)

//it is assumed that when does this that the call *should* succeed, otherwise one would use vanilla approve instead.

if(!_spender.call(bytes4(bytes32(sha3("receiveApproval(address,uint256,address,bytes)"))), msg.sender, _value, this, _extraData)) { throw; }

        return true;

    }

}

You have to throw this text in your required text editor, such as Sublime. You have to replace everything in this area where it mentions "modify these values for your own token".

It means that you will make the following changes:

Name of token

Symbol of token (can be over four characters)

Decimal places of token

Total start up as an owner

Amount of circulated tokens

Keep it in mind that the supply that you adjust for token is correlated with the amount of decimal places. For instance, if you want to a token to have zero decimal places to get 100 tokens, then your supply will be 100.

If your token are 18 decimal places and a person need 100 of these tokens, the supply could be 100. If you have a token with over 18 decimal places, you must have 100 of them and supply could be 1000000000000000000 (18 zeros are added to this amount).

You can set the number of tokens as a contract creator. The line of code will be:

Balances[message.sender] = total_number_of_tokens_mention_here

After setting, everything will be sent to ETH wallet of wherever you use the contract. You can adjust the supply of tokens. You can adjust the number of tokens to send in ETH wallet. If you need something advance, feel free to set some advanced rules like founders of projects may receive dissimilar amounts. Once you obtain variables, it is the right time to deploy it to blockchain and test.

4.3.3 Use TestNet to Test Tokens

You can deploy the contract to TestNet to see if it is working. It is difficult to deploy contract to MainNet, make payment and watch it unsuccessful. You can download MetaMask to get the advantage of their convenient interface for testing.

After installing MetaMask, you have to logged in and set up a Ropsten network for test. To reverse it to Ropsten, you can click in the upper left.

Top of a MetaMask window may look similar to this:

  METAMASK

The wallet will become the owner of a contract, so you can't lose this wallet. If you don't want MetaMask, you can get the advantage of MyEtherWallet or Mist to create contracts.

You can get the advantage of solidity compiler remix and it is one online compiler that permits you to publish a Smart Contract directly to blockchain.

You can copy and paste the contract source to modify in a main window. It will look similar to:

```
browser/ballot.sol
1   pragma solidity ^0.4.4;
2
3 - contract Token {
4
5       /// @return total amount of tokens
6       function totalSupply() constant returns (uint256 supply) {}
7
8       /// @param _owner The address from which the balance will be retrieved
9       /// @return The balance
10      function balanceOf(address _owner) constant returns (uint256 balance) {}
11
12      /// @notice send `_value` token to `_to` from `msg.sender`
13      /// @param _to The address of the recipient
14      /// @param _value The amount of token to be transferred
15      /// @return Whether the transfer was successful or not
16      function transfer(address _to, uint256 _value) returns (bool success) {}
17
18      /// @notice send `_value` token to `_to` from `_from` on the condition it is approved by `_from`
19      /// @param _from The address of the sender
20      /// @param _to The address of the recipient
21      /// @param _value The amount of token to be transferred
22      /// @return Whether the transfer was successful or not
23      function transferFrom(address _from, address _to, uint256 _value) returns (bool success) {}
24
25      /// @notice `msg.sender` approves `_addr` to spend `_value` tokens
26      /// @param _spender The address of the account able to transfer the tokens
27      /// @param _value The amount of wei to be approved for transfer
28      /// @return Whether the approval was successful or not
29      function approve(address _spender, uint256 _value) returns (bool success) {}
30
31      /// @param _owner The address of the account owning tokens
32      /// @param _spender The address of the account able to transfer the tokens
33      /// @return Amount of remaining tokens allowed to spent
34      function allowance(address _owner, address _spender) constant returns (uint256 remaining) {}
35
36      event Transfer(address indexed _from, address indexed _to, uint256 _value);
37      event Approval(address indexed _owner, address indexed _spender, uint256 _value);
38
39  }
```

You can move to settings on the right side, choose current released version of compiler, and uncheck enable optimization. It will look similar to this:

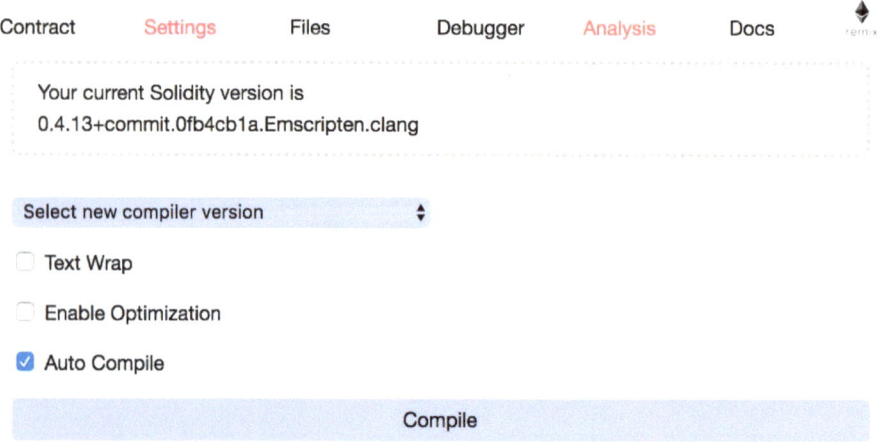

You have to manage the solidity version in a compiler. You may need this for the verification of a contract source. It is time to move back to contract tab and tap create under the name of token function you have just created. You will hit under the "Tutorial Token".

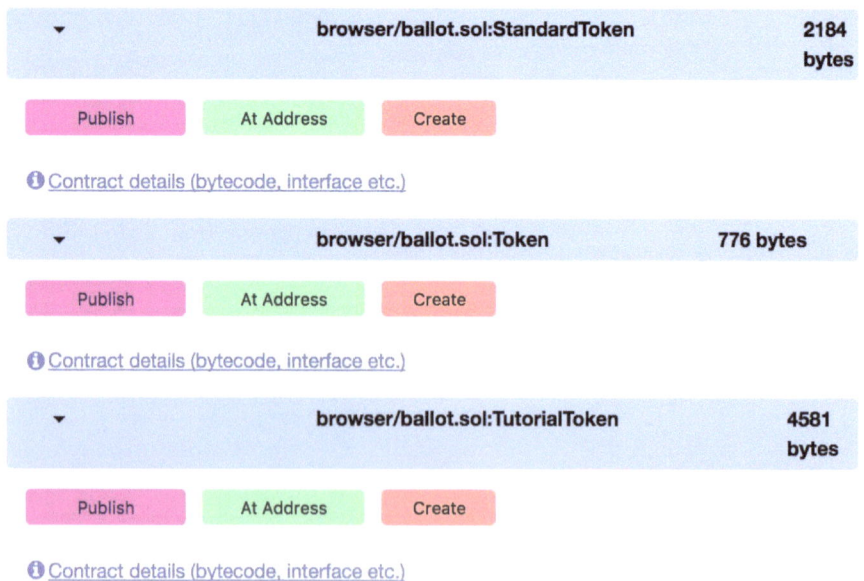

Now MetaMask will appear and ask you to tap submit for the payment of transaction. Keep it in mind that Ropsten test is not real Ether. You must double check to ensure that you are using MetaMask test network. As you hit submit, it will say that "pending contract" in MetaMask. When it will be ready, you can hit the date and it will bring a transaction in EtherScan. Similar to this:

 10    July 10 2018 13:28
Contract Published    0 ETH

After clicking the date, you can see the following display:

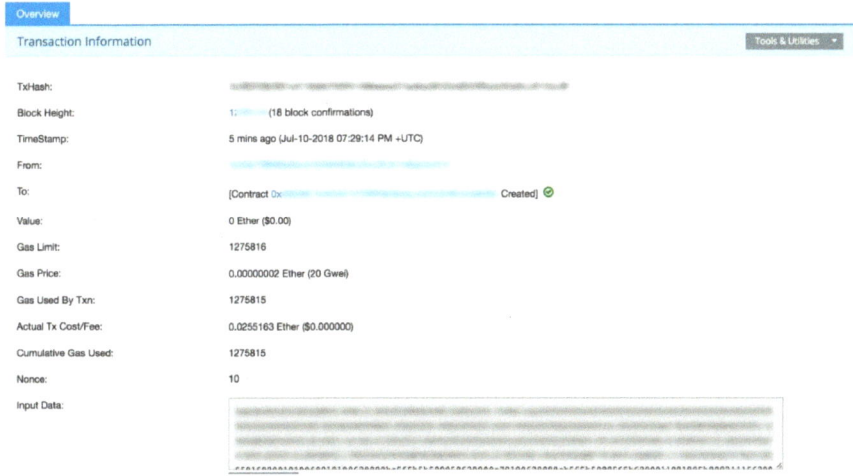

If the procedure is working, you have to verify a source code.

If the procedure is not working, you have to move back and modify this source to let it work. It is difficult to say anything about its exact look. You may have some bugs and these bugs will take lots of time to fix.

4.3.4 Custom Token

If it is actually created desired tokens and sent them to you, these may look like this:

You have to copy the address of contract mentioned in the information of transaction. Take this address and add to tokens tab of MetaMask.

SENT　　　　　　TOKENS

No Tokens Found.

When you click "+"button, you can paste the address in the given section and it will insert information of a token, similar to this:

← ADD TOKEN

Token Address

0x5...

Token Symbol

TT

Decimals of Precision

0

Add

Now you will hit add. You can get this message:

SENT   TOKENS

   100 TT

If the procedure is successful, you will get 100 tokens. Now you can send these tokens and sell them on the market.

4.3.5 Verify a Source Code

It is important for several reasons, mainly confirming the validity of token to public. It is not technically important and your token may be usable even without doing it. While noticing the transaction screen from previous step, you can click on where it claims [contract xxxx produced] in the field.

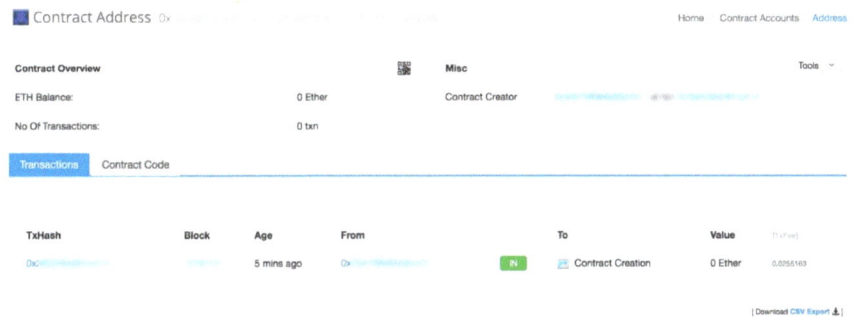

It is time to click the tab of contract code.

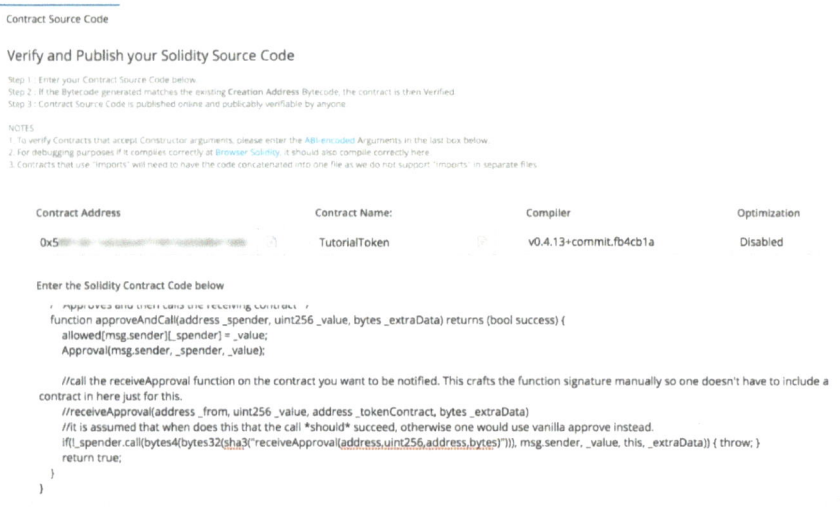

Tap "verify & publish". It will offer you this screen:

At this place, you must have the accurate settings. The address of contract will be filled in. For the name of contract, you have to mention the function that you want to modify for a custom token. The default code is ERC-20 Token, but if you want to rename it, make sure to put that as "TutorialToken".

For compiler, choose the similar compiler that you will use in a solidity compiler. Without it, you may find it difficult to verify a source code. It is important to disable optimization.

Copy and paste a code from compiler in the code field of contract. Tap submit. After doing these steps right, you can get this:

Contract Source Code   ByteCode And ABI

⊘ Note: Contract was created during Txn# [0x6c
⚠ Private Gist created for Contract source at [Online Solidity Compiler]
👍 Successfully generated ByteCode and ABI for Contract Address [0x5

It means verification.

4.3.6 On Main Net

If everything is working, you can get it on main net. This is a simple part. You have to do 3rd and 4th step instead of connected to a Test Network Ropsten. You have to connect to MainNet. Make sure to keep your MetaMask account in Mainnet mode.

You can fund you contact with original Ether. It may cost $30.

Glossary of Terms

Cryptocurrency: Any open-source cryptographically safe cryptocurrency that uses a special distributed ledger.

Legacy Financial System: Any system other than cryptocurrency system.

Cryptocurrency System: It is an accumulation of procedures and software created to enable the presence of cryptocurrencies.

Dapps (Utility-backed digital tokens): It is a decentralized digital token and its value can be derived from expediency of its uses instead of a particular value transfer system.

Pegged Cryptocurrency: A cryptocurrency whose value is pegged to the assets of real-world so it can't be considered as a utility-backed cryptocurrency.

For Top 7 ICO Rating Chart, consider this: https://twitter.com/top7ico

For Another Top 15 ICO Rating Chart, consider this: https://t.me/ico_analytic

Conclusion

ICOs are new method to increase money and everyone is attempting to adapt to new methods without being screwed over. You can create promising ICO and complete your homework in advance. Cryptocurrency have high risk and high rewards, but ICOs are similar. Investment in ICOs (initial coin offerings) and cryptocurrencies can be speculative and risk.

Acknowledge

- Raisy Chen- BitRaise Founder
- Jo-Yu Duh
- Wei-Shiun Chen

www.ingramcontent.com/pod-product-compliance
Lightning Source LLC
Chambersburg PA
CBHW040329220526
45473CB00009B/2623